Guerrilla Living

How to Live and Invest on 1,000 a
Month in the USA

Ray Chi

Guerrilla Living

How to Live and Invest on 1,000 a Month in the USA

Ray Chi

This is a Leanpub book. Leanpub empowers authors and publishers with the Lean Publishing process. Lean Publishing is the act of publishing an in-progress ebook using lightweight tools and many iterations to get reader feedback, pivot until you have the right book and build traction once you do.

Contents

Introduction

"If you're not living on the edge, you're taking up too much space." —Jack Kerouac

Who this book is for

Nearly 43 million Americans lived below the Federal Poverty Line in 2021, which is a little more than $1,000 per month. The demographics within this group are varied: they are immigrants, college students, the newly disabled. For most, their financial situation is involuntary. Is there a way to beat circumstances and get ahead? There is. Some of the strategies discussed in this book might work in the short term to free up budget or elevate quality of life.

For others, the strategies discussed in this book might inspire a new way of looking at early retirement or retirement on a fixed income.

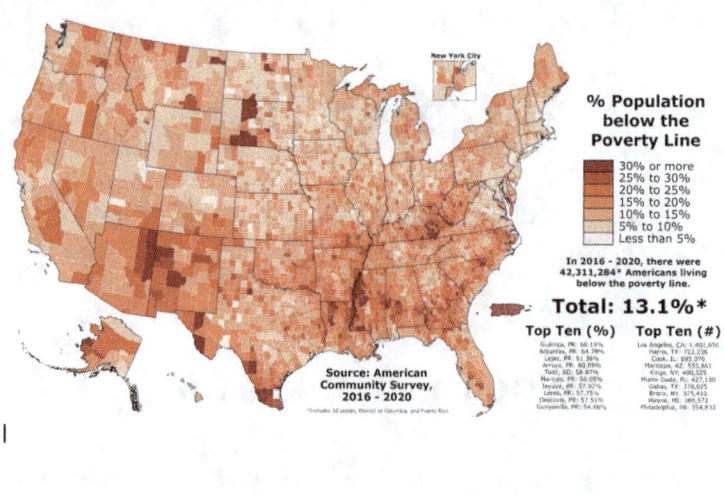

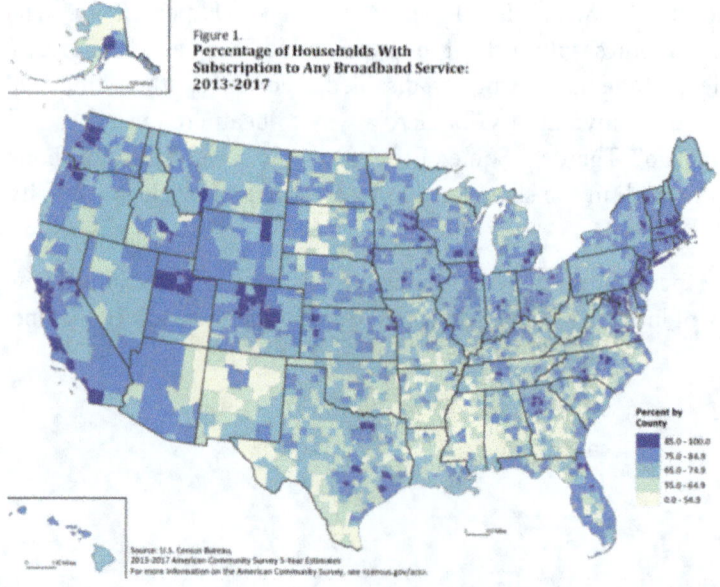

Figure 1.
Percentage of Households With Subscription to Any Broadband Service: 2013-2017

Geography and opportunity are inextricably linked. As shown in the two maps, areas with high poverty and lack of broadband internet access have high amounts of overlap. Another way to interpret the two maps is that there are huge areas of the country where people are spending *more than $1,000 per month* and *don't* have reliable high speed internet access. In a post pandemic world awash with remote opportunities - what is the resident experience in an area that doesn't have broadband internet? Access to broadband is a key metric and benchmark for *developing* countries.

The strategies in this book can work in most places, but are really designed for living within a few hours drive of a major metropolitan area to maximize the benefits offered by such areas, including broadband internet access. What benefits exist near large metros? Benefits like easy access to airports, a large tax base funding public services, and barter opportunities are important to many of the strategies in this book.

Living on $1,000 per month will not be easy but anyone following these strategies will have a good shot at having better living conditions, including better internet access. Those who are working remotely or who hold steady work could easily invest and grow their net worth while living on $1,000 per month.

This book is for more adventurous folks who are not prioritizing a career or work in general, yet want to maintain - for a year or more - their individual safety, their connection to society, and modern trappings of Western life such as:

- Access to public transportation
- Access to healthcare
- Access to government services, including police services
- Access to broadband internet
- Access to clean water
- Access to a retail supply chain

Aside from the above living standards, this book assumes no special skills or large capital up front and assumes a person does not want to spend their day doing subsistence level, physical work (i.e. walking miles to get water).

There is a chapter on "Roughing It," which is the closest to off-grid living any of the chapters gets. There are many resources and authorities available on off-grid living. In my own research, there are very few ways to do it legally without capital up front and large amounts of time doing subsistence level, physical work with specialized skills. Ditto for living a so-called "vanlife" - the up front capital necessary to live in a recreational vehicle is upwards of $20,000 and thus cost prohibitive for the average person.

However, vanlife and off grid Facebook Groups are really good online places to find barter opportunities and travel hacks for living on $1,000 per month.

Suppose you know you have $1,000 coming in monthly for life (indexed for inflation of course) and you're up for a lifestyle change.

What next? This is your book.

Minimalism

Fields Millburn and Ryan Nicodemus have a podcast on minimalism that's worth listening to. You can access the podcast from their website or Youtube free. It's part therapy, part philosophy and part downright practical advice on how to "let go" in a consumer centric society like the USA.

Importantly, minimalism is not just about managing physical things, but about living in a minimalist way. Minimalism is all about encouraging people to reclaim their time and meaning by getting rid of excess stuff and focusing on what's important. By reading this book, you may have already decided that you want to own your finances, your time, and your life and as Millburn and Nicodemus would say 'let the rest go'. Let me be more direct if you challenge your assumptions on *who* pays what and *when* your life could look very different.

A big part of living on a $1,000 monthly budget is buying exactly what you need after heavy introspection on what you really value, which is a core tenet of minimalism. A simple way to start is to just let things sit in your online shopping cart for a few weeks and let the influence of buying it pass. Often times, it does. It's also important to pay attention to the prices you are paying, which is easy to ignore when all it takes is one click to place an order.

Learn to identify the factors of influence that drive your purchasing and other life decisions. In *Influence*, Robert Cialdini explains these factors with interesting studies to show that social proof and other factors are working on you everyday to shape your decision making in ways you can barely detect.

Photo courtesy of Tania Melnyczuk / Unsplash

Buying the best priced item might mean buying used items or in some cases, taking advantage of a venture capitalist or tech company where they are lowering the price to grab market share. For example, in San Francisco there was a company called Chariot which was essentially a group ride in a van that was faster and cheaper than public transportation. It, along with other 'mommy apps' like laundry services, closed within a few years but users got a deal.

 There are many goods available for free. There are Facebook Groups dedicated to "free piles" and community exchanges at the county and city level. Often times the best strategy is to visit the 'seller' and just ask for other things for free that you see.

Buying fewer things is not only good for your budget but it's also good for the environment. Each purchase of a new item sends out a ripple effect of released carbon by a global supply chain. Some countries where goods are made take advantage of their workers and use child labor in the manufacturing process.Foxconn has suicide nets in place at their manufacturing plants[1]

---

[1]https://www.theguardian.com/world/2010/may/28/foxconn-plant-china-deaths-suicides

The following items are a short list of goods we all buy, and some ideas for how to do it cheaply:

- Smart phones: Smart phones can cost upwards of $1,000 if purchased new or financed through your cell phone service. Instead, consider buying a used, pre-inspected phone with a 30 day warranty. That would save $20-30/mo over 5 years. Also, if you have a chromebook or iPad, consider whether you even need a phone, as calls can be placed through either device.
- Clothing and shoes: Buying quality goods used (top brands that use real leather), will save you over fast fashion. Another $50/mo+ of savings here. Look to eBay or Mercari, Poshmark, or the Real Real.
- Computers/laptops. Instead of buying a new one for upwards of $2,000, consider buying used. I have bought Dell XPS 13s for $200 on ebay.

 Warranties are important, particularly for a used device. You can get warranties included free on used devices through sites like Swappa

- Subscription services: Subscriptions to everything from movie channels to gyms eat up hundreds of dollars each month.

Instead of using your actual credit card, consider using a service like Privacy.com to create a virtual credit card that kills the subscription payment after X months or X dollars and you'll see way less funneled away to unused subscriptions. The virtual credit card is only allowed to be charged a certain number of times, or months, or to a predetermined amount or by a specific vendor. You can make any number of virtual cards you want for free. Once the vendor exceeds a threshold you choose, the payment no longer goes through and you don't have to hunt down and cancel the subscription since the subscription service does not have direct access to your card. Another $20/mo of savings here.

Being aware of privacy leaks can save you money. More than one website has been caught charging Mac users more based on fingerprints left by their devices.

 Privacy.com ensures your transaction history can not be correlated with your identity or browsing history. You will see less ads and be targeted across fewer mediums if you guard your privacy leading to less expenditures.

- You might already be spending more than $1,000 a month. All expenditures should be on a cash rewards card getting you 2% back on everything. I like the Fidelity card as the cash goes straight to a brokerage account. That's another $20/mo. And no foreign transaction or ATM fees on the debit card.
- Less meat. I love steak, but I keep it to a few times a month max. Meat is an expensive and absolute water and carbon hog to get to my table and you and I, and everyone on the planet pays for it. That's another $20-50/mo. Instead, consider eating more beans and tofu, which costs far less. Embracing minimalism using the strategies discussed here will go a long way toward helping a person live on $1,000 per month.

Barter Opportunities

Photo courtesy of Unsplash

This is going to be a short chapter for a reason so I'll mention my own personal experience. When I lived in San Francisco, I had a small dog and travelled fairly often. Due to the location of the apartment (Nob Hill), it was easy for me to find dog sitters who would sit the dog in exchange for staying at my place. Hotels in the area were charging two to three times the daily price of what paying a dog sitter would cost me. This was, in effect, a *great* deal for both the sitter and myself. Some sitters were retirees flying in to visit their kids who were attending local universities. Bartering their pet sitting duties in exchange for a free stay meant that these retirees were able to stay for free in a major metropolitan area like San Francisco.

Pet sitting can also yield savings in the long term, as it did for one couple I knew. They worked full time as pet sitters in the Bay Area, while commuting to their full time jobs in San Francisco. This allowed them to live rent free for *years*. This strategy works best for those who: 1) can pass a background check on one of the popular pet sitting websites that connect owners with sitters, 2) live in a large enough city where there is high demand for sitters and 3) have a smartphone and internet access. The smartphone is necessary as many owners require frequent "pup-dates" or updates consisting of photos taken of their pets throughout the day and sent in real time to the owner. A car might also be necessary if you want to expand your reach to the wider suburban areas of large cities. It goes without saying that you have to be respectful and careful with the owner's home and belongings. Post-pandemic, pet sitting is in high demand. Don't be a jerk and drink all the pet owner's whiskey. No joke this happened to me once, but I didn't complain since the sitter was incredibly good at taking pup-dates.

There are many other bartering opportunities besides pet sitting. For example, there are "work-trade"specific websites you can query for opportunities to barter work in exchange for housing and meals and many seasonal jobs listed on these sites provide longer term housing- hello Jackson Hole! There are seasonal work programs for fire control and invasive plant management that effectively blend real service with great outdoor opportunities. Becoming a part time caretaker, groundskeeper or au pair is also a form of barter, but are much harder to find without considerable hours.

The caretaker option, specifically only a night shift to care for an older person, is ideal as you get a free place to stay with amenities without any of the hassle of doing errands and appointments. With the right training (basic first AID, vitals), caretaking can quickly turn into a highly paid position depending on the senior you're taking care of. The night shift barter opportunity is highly in demand in high cost of living cities where the cost of daytime care is exorbitant.

Similarly, small apartment landlords can also be a source of live in property management/custodial gigs where not a lot of work is done in exchange for free rent.

Urban hostels are always looking for help and can offer accommodation. Hostels need help checking in guests, managing bookings, and light janitorial work that is frequently done at night.

X takes up a night shift caretaker gig 5 nights a week and pet sits 2 nights a week. X gets rid of the car but relies on Uber and public transport more.

	Pre	Post
Rent	$2500	$0
Car	$1000	$0
Other Expenses	$2500	$1700
Total	$6000	$1700

Share and Subdivide

When you bought this book, you were probably racing to critique a budget to see the 'how' of living on $1,000 a month would work. We'll get to sample budgets, but the most important consideration is where those dollars are sourced from. Does it matter if you spend $4,000 a month and only $1,000 are contributed by you?

Sharing and subdividing your housing is an important way to reduce your living expenses, but also, to generate revenue. Peer to peer platforms like Airbnb and Getaround have turned sharing opportunities into business opportunities that can get you to a $1,000 net monthly. Your expenses on paper might be more than $1,000 per month, because your rent or mortgage is higher than that, but you're off-setting your expenses with revenue - living off the excess - and really contributing only $1,000 toward your expenses.

This means you can provide yourself housing, make money, and own your time albeit with some liabilities. The main liabilities are your time spent to manage the activity, your deposit and the value of things you or your guests have in the unit. Sharing websites usually provide a short term insurance policy to cover the guest's stay and have a way to compensate the guest if the unit is not available (i.e. can't check in or last minute cancellation by you or your designated host).

Sharing is going to be the most immediate way to drive costs down quickly and by mixing lifestyle strategies in this book (i.e house sits, boat share, roughing it, foreign travel, etc...) you can more easily blend your lifestyle with your new $1,000 budget.

This chapter will get a lot of eye rolls for obviousness especially if you're already sharing all you have. Sharing and subdividing, repeatedly, is often enough to get you close to a $1,000 monthly budget.

However, if you add leverage (hard money loans, multiple leases,etc...) you can easily net much more than living rent free.

 Focus on the big ticket items first to get quick gains

Rent is the first thing you should share as it's likely 30% or more of your take home i.e. after tax income and is in demand *everywhere*, at least everywhere that meets the criteria in this book. Share your existing space with short or long term roommates.

In Manhattan, it's quite common for college students to subdivide small apartments using airwalls. An airwall is a temporary wall that is quickly erected with the look and feel of real drywall - you can hang a shelf, for example. Think of an air mattress but on its side that makes a wall.

Short term roommates are more profitable. In popular vacation areas or business travel destinations (Miami Beach, San Francisco, New York City), one can usually pay several months rent just off renting a few days during a few events - Ultra Music fest, Dreamforce for example. Events are not limited to major cities. For example, Derby brings short term rental opportunities to Louisville for example. The same short term high gain opportunity exists in college towns, where events such as reunions, homecoming, or football games means that a house or apartment in close proximity to the event can be rented out for a weekend for the equivalent of the monthly rent.

One way to maximize this strategy is to use your profits to put down deposits and get more apartments in your name. There are entrepreneurs that effectively rezone apartment units into hotel type accommodations in San Francisco with this strategy and pulling in six figure side incomes.

You can even co-sign a lease to help someone *else* secure leases, and run this strategy for you for passive income until you switch over to full time passive income. There is an entire cottage industry dedicated to automating short term rental operations. For example, Vacasa will provide 24/7 guest service, ensure the unit is turned over, and manage all disputes for you. Several turnkey services exist and there are sites that provide training on rental arbitrage like BNB University and pricing data to help you evaluate opportunities for sub-leasing. If you have multiple properties in one city, it'd very easy to live in them during vacancies.

Again, the goal here is to get a usable space to live while spending only $1,000 per month on yourself even if you're spending multiples of that on everything else with other people's money.

Everyone has different risk tolerances and having multiple leases out may not be for you. There are other ways to share what you own or rent. If you have access to an attractive yard, for instance, you could put a yurt in it and rent it out. Or you could live in it and profit off your sub-leased tenants with the right property and tenant profile. Another idea is to rent out the yard for catered events, such as a wedding. Maximizing the use of your driveway for rentable parking space also works if you are near a stadium, ballpark or other public venue, including seasonal ones such as art fairs or festivals. Again, you should evaluate these opportunities before you sign a lease or buy a house, as you would with any investment's cash flow potential.

House hacking

House hacking is essentially using sub-dividing or other strategies to accelerate wealth creation through home ownership. Sub-dividing involves creating temporary divisions in already used space or monetizing unused space. Unlike sharing, the space is altered physically or altered functionally in some way. For example, mostly everyone has electricity, and traveling RV'ers need a spot to refill water and recharge batteries. A neighbor of mine just put in a parking space for RVs and no doubt wrote off their investment while improving the value of their home. Dividing a space out in your garage for an RV could be another way to lower your monthly living expense

When you write off a business expense, you reduce taxable income from that activity. But what people forget is that there's no rule that an activity ever be profitable and many ventures are not. So that expense really becomes a larger tax refund (if you pay taxes) as the business expense will create a loss against your other forms of income, such as W2 income.

In parts of California, Accessory Dwelling Unit permits are "ministerially approved" i.e they are fast tracked and can be installed with pre-fabricated kits for under $300/sq ft. My lower deck is completely useless to me - it's far from the rest of the house yet if it were enclosed it would be 500 sq ft of space that I could rent out for $1500. If you're lucky enough to be able to buy a home, buy one with enough space on the lot to build more or better yet, one with an existing in-law unit.

 • HipCamp and other online platforms will connect you with campers and RVers in need of space.

Subdividing raw unimproved land with the *right* zoning and road access is also feasible for renting to glampers and the RV crowd. Each county has its own zoning requirements, but in general the goal here is to keep the use in line with zoning - most jurisdictions restrict mobile home and RV park development. One or two RVs can be parked on residential lots. Agricultural or commercial zoning is much more permissive. The Overlander app provides a good tool to research demand for RV routes.

As we'll see in Roughing It, raw land is more affordable than you think.

Consider travel networks like couchsurfing.com and Servas for open spots in your city to take advantage of how others are providing sub-divided resources for you to consume for free.

Your car is probably your next biggest expense after real estate and your most expensive asset, and 90% of the time it's unused. If you can't get rid of it, online platforms like Turo and Getaround may be available to help you rent it out and reduce your operating expense. If these apps are not available there's nothing stopping you from securing your own insurance rider and just renting your vehicle out. There's a lot more work and risk to renting out cars, but for the right car and the right location peer to peer car rental is profitable. For example, if there is a break down or a lockout you might have to be on-call to help the renter out. The work is mostly in cleaning the vehicle and doing proper inspections post rental to cover damages. A major risk here is that the insurance process to get a claim paid out can take months for damage caused by a renter. Always factor the tax benefits of paper losses in your analysis here as they can easily be a large percentage of your economic profit if you pay income taxes on other income. People generally are unaware of bonus depreciation rules, which effectively get you a write off of 50-80% of the value of the property *up front*.

You could extend the sharing concept to other equipment you own or even to your cash savings (i.e. peer to peer lending on Lend-ingClub), but typically that's capital intensive and is considerable work. In peer to peer lending, you're essentially lending out your capital (your savings) at interest rates higher than corporate bonds and less than credit cards and receiving no collateral. The risk of default is reduced by the ability to lend small amounts ($50) to many borrowers across different credit scores. You can also sell your loans before the borrowers are done paying up to get all your cash back or even at a premium if interest rates drop. The work involved is considerable - you have to learn the platform and get ahead of the big players who are already getting access to top borrowers on the platforms.

You can even share your body fluids. I donated plasma twice a week for two years in college and received up to $100 a week for time in a lounge chair watching TV.

Whether you use these strategies to get your total expenses to below $1,000 or to generate income and tax advantages it doesn't matter.

So let's do quick table to illustrate pre-and post share and subdivide:

	Pre	Post
Rent	$2500	$-500
Car	$1000	$300
Other Expenses	$2500	$1500
Total	$6000	$1300

In this scenario, X quits his job. Before quitting, X rents and subleases a 3BD house (2 rooms rented and the 3rd room for

AirBnB) in the suburbs ditching the $2500 studio. The 3rd room is rented 30% of the time and profits $500/mo. X eliminates the car preferring to use ride apps, public transportation and bicycling. X now buys less things (because he has less space to put them) and has reduced utilities to just a cell phone. Other Expenses are increased by AirBnb expenses, a boat share (more on that later) which X is able to use as a place to sleep 3 nights a week. The boat is parked at night alternately at the marina and out in protected waters (i.e. in front of the marina) when slept in. X still has an occasional night to accommodate for, which X can easily do with the next strategy.

Roughing It

By now you've probably realized that a nomadic lifestyle, while saving you tens of thousands on rent, is a lot of planning and movement. So why not incorporate a chill out week?

Photo courtesy of Karson Chan / Unsplash

Every year billions are spent on outdoor equipment and campground fees. You may or not be one of the millions that sleep outside and pay for the luxury every year. If you've never camped or backpacked before, you'll be surprised that it can actually cost more money per day to sleep outside in private campsites and public parks than it does to just sleep at home when entrance fees and gear rental are factored in. Campsites in the Florida Keys or coastal California are reserved months, even years in advance and in many cases cost more than low range hotels in the same market do during the *same* time.

So while some of this chapter may seem like advocating periodic homelessness (it's not), there's a very different perspective from marketers, professional guides, and tens of thousands of park employees on 'sleeping outside' with a lot of money and eyeballs on it.

Dominic Van Allen[1]lived beneath one of London's busiest parks for 7 years. He had standing room in his living space, two beds, a stove and a concrete floor. He maintained cover by adhering to "operational security" - always accessing the space in the dark, not cooking smelly foods, etc...and building it in the dark with tools that were submerged and out of sight by dawn. He was only found out when the bushes near the entrance were cleared out and steam was emanating from his entrance on a winter day. Dominic's story shows us one can live for free for extended periods of time in cosmopolitan cities by following basic measures.

The West

Although camping in reserved campsites can cost a bundle, consider camping on Federal and state lands that are not designated as parks. They are surprisingly accessible. For example, did you know that 50% of California is owned by the Federal government? Aside from military bases, this means you have access to a lot of land in California and much of the West since it's Federal land (Nevada is almost 80% Federal). Aside from Alaska, there is no other state with more acreage designated as wilderness than California.

You can generally camp in Forest Service and BLM lands in dispersed camping for 14 consecutive days and the clock restarts when you leave the park.

---

[1]https://www.theguardian.com/news/2020/mar/05/invisible-city-how-homeless-man-built-life-underground-bunker-hampstead-heath

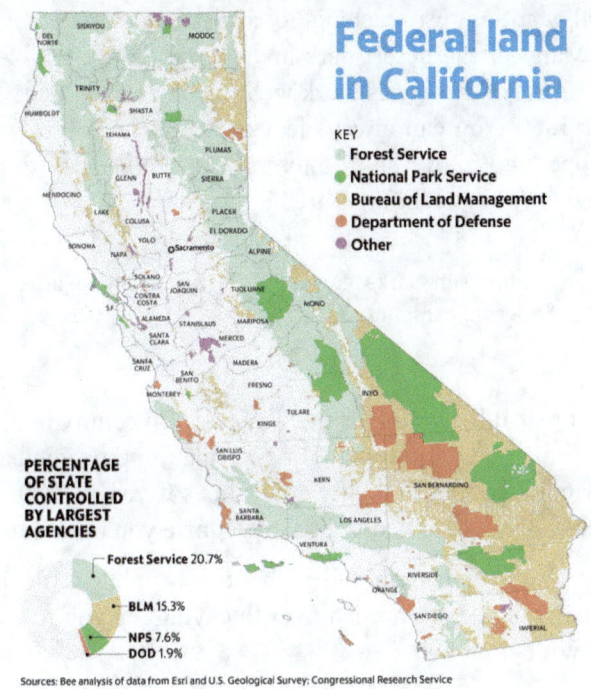

Figure 1. California Federal Lands Map

Obviously, some areas are highly seasonal due to wildfire and snow pack. Several areas are serviced by public transportation and are within an hour of a major city.

In general, broadband internet is available to mobile devices in wilderness areas throughout the southern portion of the state and the Bay Area. Higher ridges have better cell signal.

Due to the distances from BLM land to the coast and larger cities, it's harder to mix Roughing It in BLM California with other strategies (house share, boats) so time roughing it might be spent in longer increments on Federal land. Some state parks like Anza Borrego near the Salton Sea have generous 30 day per year caps on camping that are of course nearly impossible to actually enforce.

You will want to use caching to distribute supplies and even water. Many of the desert park areas have springs and seasonal creeks. Used Pelican boxes work well for cache sites since they're weatherproof. You can always leave a map in one box with the actual topo map to overlay it on a map in *another* box to remind you of where your cache sites are.

 County run parks generally are too small to offer dispersed camping.

Guerilla or stealth camping is the way to go on county land unless you pay for a hard to find spot. For guerrilla camping you basically have to look like a local jogger at all times if you're there during the week as the staff will definitely recognize you over time.

I don't recommend camping illegally or near public infrastructure as again, if your experience isn't worth paying for, you're probably doing it wrong.

The East

On the East Coast, although less land is owned by the Federal government than in the West, there are national forests such as the White Mountains National Forest in New Hampshire and Maine where free dispersed camping is available. There are also numerous state forests consisting of millions of acres of scenic land available for (free) dispersed camping and are a short train or bus ride away from major metropolitan areas such as New York, Baltimore, Philadelphia, Washington D.C. and Boston.

For most of these, there are no entry fees or permit requirements, and campers have been observed to stay for a season in these backcountry sites, many of them waterfront on the numerous ponds and lakes in the park. During winter in the East, camping in coastal state forests is the way to go. These are located in eleven states along the eastern seaboard, such as Florida, Alabama, North Carolina, Virginia, and Maryland. You can snag a prime waterfront site and fishing and crabbing are permitted.

The Appalachian Trail

James Hammes stole $8M dollars from his employer and disappeared in 2006. He evaded the FBI for six years while living on the Appalachian Trail (AT). James adopted the trail name 'Bismarck' and was only caught when someone who had travelled with him on the trail saw an episode of American Greed. James' story shows how even an FBI fugitive can live quite comfortably for years and very sociably by Roughing It. It's not clear how much he spent while living on the trail, but he did agree to pay back most of what he stole. But you don't need to be a fugitive to get the cost savings of spending a month or two backpacking if you are fit enough to do it.

The AT is a very popular trail that runs 2,200 miles from Georgia to Maine. It has challenging terrain in some parts and takes so long to complete that hikers arrange for supplies to be mailed to specific drop points- a strategy you will see later. There are shelters along the way and trailheads have nearby inns and towns that cater to through hikers. In fact, you are never more than a day's hike from a warm bed. There are also 'trail fairies' who take in and feed hikers. Water access is easy and so is fast internet. In general, it is much wetter, more populated, and easier to complete than the longer Pacific Crest Trail.

There are 20+ lesser known trail systems (aka 'through hikes') that are worth exploring like the Pacific Northwest trail and Minnesota Lake trails.

The Bounce Box

If you never leave your city, you can disregard this tip. The US Post Office will store your stuff rent free for up to two weeks in most locations before sending it back. So what through hikers do is send a box of necessities that are useless on trail (such as a battery charger) to their next location and time their walk so that the box arrives and isn't turned back by the time they arrive at the new post office. You could also just use Amazon or a mail forwarder to send you exactly what you need straight to a park or local Amazon locker.

A clever move would be to rotate seasonally through California using bounce boxes. In winter, you might get a lot of pet sitting gigs in San Francisco around the holidays and you send your gear to a post office near a desert park or the park itself when folks return after the holidays. You then camp out in the desert for a week or two. You send the box back to your city post office when you're done. You head down to Baja California for a week or so and then pick the box back up when you're at another gig in the city.

Let's look at a sample winter monthly budget with bounce box rotation where you spend 5 days a month in Baja.

Your $1,000 in other monthly expenses are:

1. Seasonal gear rental $100
2. Food $400 while camping and in Baja
3. Transport to and from parks and Baja including airfare $500
4. Bounce Box Postage $100
5. Misc: $100

	Pre	Post
Rent	$2500	$150
Car	$1000	$0
Other Expenses	$2500	$1200
Total	$6000	1350

Opsec

Basic operational security should be adhered to wherever you rough it:

- Isolate. Keep valuables and food away from where you sleep so if the sleep site is found by humans or animals your stuff is ok. A raised tent and campsite with items strewn everywhere is a dead giveaway.
- Always have a pretext for why you're there and look the part, with little on you. Binoculars and a field/astronomy guide, jogging clothing, etc..
- Defense in depth. Have backup caches and sites with redundant supplies.
- Use a red film over your phone at night to keep bright screens from giving you away
- Be gone in the day and approach at dusk/dawn.
- Approach your site in a J pattern so that you'll spot any followers before arriving at your site
- Plan on blending in using a gilly net or natural materials for cover
- No visitors
- Avoid fires or learn to make a Dakota fire
- Leave no trace
- Build out your space over time setting up cache sites.

Why cache sites? You want to travel light to fit your pretext and conserve budget. One can literally travel between SFO and the desert on Spirit in the same day for under $100.

There are several designs of lean to's that are quick to build, blend in and are fairly weather proof.

Roughing it is not propping up a tent in an alley or under a freeway where you're at the mercy of the streets. Drug addicts and the mentally ill do it to conserve energy.

A one man tent or tarp and line combo is still likely to be the fastest structure to prop up and keep concealed compared to a thatch hut or similar so no need to go Rambo. Also many parks forbid cutting vegetation.

The goal here is to have *multiple* places you can comfortably spend a night that are still close enough to storage and a shower. You're not homeless, you're sleeping outside for the night and having fun doing it. I highly recommend joining stealth camping Facebook Groups for inspiration and tips.

Living outside for a night or two stealthily is easier in topographies that feature mountains for concealment and oceans to moderate temperatures.

Life Underground

Over one million people live underground in sanctioned housing in China. These 'shuzu' or rat people are mostly students looking to pay half price on rent. There is an entire town living in an opal mine in Australia called Coober Peddy. Native Americans (Pueblos near the Gila River) and contemporary Americans do live in caves today (Ozarks) but few would have access to healthcare and police services.

There are underground dwellers in New York's unused Amtrack line and hundreds living in Las Vegas' storm drain system.

I am not recommending living in public infrastructure underground as you don't really have access to police services or the internet or clean water. In fact, most denizens who live like this don't want to be found.

To really pull this off you'd have to be within a populated metro area and dig something out over time yourself for safety like Dominic did in London.

Buy Some Dirt

Bid4assets.com is a website used by counties and agencies to auction defaulted or seized property. There are others like land-watch.com and even Facebook marketplace where rural lots in the desert and forested areas with road access, within 30 min drive of major parks in some cases, routinely go for less than $2,000 per lot. Zoning is a lot more permissive in rural areas particularly in red states. I have seen lots 45 minutes from Las Vegas airport with utilities on street (which you really don't need given solar potential) for less than $2,000. There are unbuildable lots in Humboldt County with *ocean* views for under $7,000 that will allow a tiny home or RV with no foundation and *nothing* else. Even if your lot is zoned residential with nosy neighbors, you could subdivide or rent to travelling RVs if you're close to a major RV route. States like Florida and Arizona have RV friendly jurisdictions everywhere.

What would you do with an empty lot in a rural area? You'd live in it seasonally and explore the area. One could feasibly pay to have a camper trailer (pop top) towed onto your own lot where you could live in it seasonally and rent it out when you're not there. You could also charge others to park their RVs there.

Even in California, you could build a 10 x 12 tool shed with no permit and outfit it with low voltage DC, a composting toilet, a water barrel and you're in business - just look on AirBnbs near major national parks for inspiration.

If you're serious about building but want to do it cheaply, you have to look at earthbag building.

Photo courtesy of Saeed Ketabi / Unsplash

In earthbag building, your materials are literally right underneath you. All you need is a shovel, nylon bags, a few tools and barbed wire and you can make a very sound, very energy efficient 10 x 12 structure by yourself within a week. Folks have built earthbag structures and stayed warm in single digit temps outside with very basic heating. The construction advantages are enormous - dirt is free, no transporting materials in or powered equipment needed and there is no concern about insulation.

Of course, if you want a secure door, cabinets, electricity and water (and maybe a graywater setup) you'll need hand tools and materials to build and transport to get it all there. Experience from a basic woodshop class would really help here. The building technique, well known to the military for ages, was pioneered by Nader Khalil in the 1970s and his organization CalEarth, and several others, teach classes on earthbag building in the Great Basin Desert.

Squats, Weed Farms, Communes and Slab City

Slab City in south-eastern California is considered to be one of the last free places in the United States. Despite the free love vibe, you are in the middle of the desert on an abandoned military base far from any services.

Photo courtesy of Olga DeLawrence / Unsplash

Major safety concerns or missing criteria. Avoid.

Outside Lands

Up until now you've probably asked yourself 1) why is X paying nearly half their monthly income on rent and 2) what is $2500 of other expenses a month, really? Well, no one spends an exact same amount each month and baked in to the $2500 of other expenses is the assumption that you're annualizing your costs (i.e. you spend $6k on travel a year which is $500/mo of the $2500) and that prices are consistently that high, because you're in the *same* place.

The same place being an expensive city like San Francisco.

But you don't have to be in the *same* place. And maybe you spend $2,000 per month while you're living somewhere more expensive, but it averages out over the year.

We tend to think there's one price for a good, like gasoline. Maybe there's small price adjustments based on the gas station's location or the brand but the price per gallon (for the same type of gas) is generally similar between gas stations on the same road. The moment you start to relax certain attributes, like location, all of a sudden there's more than one price. Gas prices can vary by 50% or more between California and other states.

Things get more interesting when you introduce currency types.

Before going further I'm going to explain what purchasing power parity (PPP) is, the effect of market exchange rates, and why price levels matter. PPP is just another form of an exchange rate. The PPP between the U.S. dollar and another currency is the exchange rate that would be required to purchase the same quantity of the same goods and services locally that cost $1 in the United States. PPP is what drives the advantage to moving overseas - not only do you get 20 pesos for 1 USD, but it only costs you .50 USD in Mexico, which has a PPP of 10, to buy what $1 in America could buy.

You can think of the price level as the ratio of PPP to market exchange rates. PPP attempts to equalize the cost of a basket of goods, priced in different currencies. Exchange rates change in the short run and don't accurately reflect actual changes in standards of living in short time periods. When GDP per capita on PPP is higher than GDP based on exchange rates for a particular country, as it is in Mexico, it indicates that the country has a lower price level than the United States.

Mexico is an obvious destination as the PPP and weather is much better than in Canada and a good part of the country is a short flight or even walkable from the States. If you're ok with distance, your money will go much farther in South East Asia or Indonesia than in Mexico as the PPP's are even lower.

If all this is too complicated for you, check out the Big Mac index from *The Economist*, which clearly shows the same Big Mac is $3.30 USD in Mexico and over $5 in California. Basically, you're getting ripped off because you live in a higher price level country. Make sense?

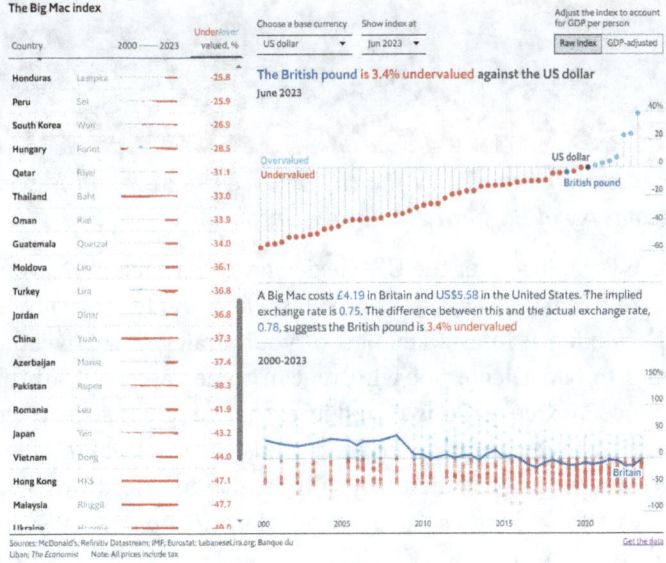

Baja

The border wall between in the surf between the US and Mexico. Photo courtesy of Barbara Zandoval / Unsplash

Northern Baja, just over the US-Mexico border from San Diego, is a broke retiree paradise. It's also so close to the States you *have* to consider mixing it in as a key part of your strategy. The weather is similar to San Diego, but with rent in some cases at 1/4th the price. Since Mexico's PPP is 10 and its exchange rate is 20 its prices are going to be lower for non-traded goods such as local food and labor. No need to drive here – you'll be able to afford ride apps and buses all day long as the average Tijuana employee working 'formal work' makes just $360 USD a month. For what it's worth, Northern Baja has income inequality so the highest 10% are making much more than that. Depending on who you, as a non-Spanish speaker are talking to, you could get a different perception on cost.

The first time I went to Baja I was shocked at how some of the neighborhoods looked like postage stamp communities in the States and had nothing but California license plates driving around. The area has a thriving dental and pharma trade for medical tourists from the US as millions of Americans don't have medical or dental coverage. Americans quickly find out that any medical or dental procedure *actually has a price*, which ironically American's are unaccustomed to. Also, procedures can be performed more cheaply than in the States by reputable doctors and dentists in state of the art medical facilities.

In some beach towns, expats are nearly a third of the population. Particularly good values on rentals and real estate can be found just an hour inland from the coast. Northern Baja is actually considered to be expensive compared to other parts of Mexico.

Moving just across the border was ultimately what my family member did since it was the easiest and simplest of all the options. I met Corey well after completing my family member's move, and asked him a few questions about his experience.

ExPats in Tijuana Mexico
Corey Oz · July 7 · 🌐   ···

I moved out of DE in 2015 and until 2018 I lived in Vegas, on a cruise ship in Hawaii and SD. 5 years ago this month I was forced out of SD due to rising rental prices and my foolish optimism. That same foolish optimism sent me to MX and as it turns out, had been the greatest experience of my life by a mile. I feel freer, I need only 1 job and it's part time, SENTRI and strong discipline. Tijuana had convinced me to never return to live in the US and to one day move farth... **See more**

 You and 229 others   73 comments

👍 Like   💬 Comment   ➢ Send

I am sure things are different now then when you first moved over. What did you feel you had to improve, if anything since you moved?

I moved to Tijuana accidentally -I moved to SD from Delaware and over time SD rent got expensive and so it was on to TJ. The first two months I was thinking it was too good to be true. I had to work on that, my attitudes and expectations around how I'd be treated.

I was about two months in when I got my first utility bill from my landlord - wifi, electric, gas all in...it was $5 USD. From that point on I knew this was real I was all in. I also had to deal with some guilt about that.

What level of connection with the US do you have and why do you still keep it?

I work as a bartender in SD. So I do a 3hr round trip 2-5 days a week part time. I also go to SD to visit family, friends in town. I also have my mail and doctors and stuff in the US. It's just easier since I work there and I want to keep it all simple. Long term when I become financially independent I'm going to cut ties and just move South.

Aside from financial savings, do you see any other benefits of the move?

I used to have two jobs. I was able to cut one out and living here really opened up my options as to what I want to do for work. I have a job I want versus an extra one I need. The other thing is I just have a sense of fellowship here - the cultural difference is really big even though SD is visible, it's you know right there but its a big change - I just have more faith in humanity and this has really empowered me. I got all that by taking a really small risk a lot of Americans can take.

What fear did you have to get over?

I had to change my attitude around racism. I had questions about dealing with racism or just knowing the rules, but those concerns didn't really materialize.

What would you tell someone thinking of making the move?

Not everyone can do this - if you've got a serious illness, handicap, a lot of stuff you want to bring over, kids, a criminal background - that complicates things. Other than that you can live on $1k/USD without an issue. You need to be willing to take a small risk.

Retiree Visa

A Mexican retiree visa is only needed if you want to stay more than six months at a time. If you plan on purchasing property or running a business you'll want to pursue a full residency permit. Staying six months continuously on the Mexican side is unlikely, as living so close to the border you'll inevitably cross over for a doctor's appointment or to pick up food stamps and mail at your mailbox rental where you can reset the clock and obtain a new 'FMM' - a permit to stay six months, if you bother. The cost for the six month FMM visa purchased at the border is less than $30 as of 2023 and is only really needed if you travel a certain distance from the border, such as to Cancun or other parts of Mexico via air travel. You'll want to keep your state residency if you're American to qualify for state level and local benefits, like free cell phones. If you lose your passport, you can re-enter the US with any ID and your social security number in emergency situations. There's a passport agency off the Blue Line in San Diego where you can replace your passport in a few hours.

Lodging

By far the best way to score your own apartment under $400 per month is to walk around neighborhoods and inquire, but deals can be had if you scour Facebook groups and search in Spanish on sites in pesos. You can also just grab an AirBnb and just work something out. Don't ever reveal your true budget. You might need an 'aval' (type of cosigner) to secure a lease of your own apartment.

The price post pandemic has increased greatly as more folks have retired sooner. The price has continued to rise as many pandemic movers actually stayed and just decided to work remotely or part time. You often hear about illegal immmigrants coming to America on the news, but you don't see pictures of the miles long line of American's crossing over to Mexico every day.

Internet & Money

Get a Telcel sim card on Amazon and just refill it every so often online. You'll then have data and a local phone number - good public wifi can be a challenge to find. The Telcel sim cards work on the US side so you'll be able to hail an Uber and call just as with a US sim card. You can send money to yourself using Remitly and pick it up in 7-Elevens,Walmart, and thousands of other locations in Mexico with just an ID and a pin. Certain banks, like Charles Schwab and Fidelity, cover international ATM fees and don't charge foreign transaction fees either.

Border Crossings

You can cross by foot and be on the San Ysidro trolley (Blue Line) in San Diego in less than an hour from parts of Tijuana, but expect at least a one hour wait in line going back to the US and longer during peak commute hours. The trolley is 50 yards from the border wall at the San Ysidro crossing. Other border crossings like Otay and Tecate are faster but do not have the same trolley on the other side but do have Uber. The Tijuana airport has its own crossing in the airport itself. Entering the US can have multi hour waits if you're in a car. There is a Sentri pass, similar to Global Entry, that can significantly speed things up. If you have to cross more than once a week in a car the pass is a good idea.

Driving

No need for your own car in Mexico. Just pay a local to drive you and have a few backup drivers. There are many Americans who offer 'concierge' like services where they drive you to the border, you get out and walk over with your stuff, and they pick you up on the American side to do errands by car in San Diego. Typical fares to 'La Garita' - the border wall- are $20-$30 from as far south as Rosarito and just a few dollars if using shared vanpools. Border crossings are easier on foot or on bike. Driving exposes you to scams, police corruption and dangerous road conditions at night which will eat into your $1,000 per month budget.

Tijuana and Rosarito

X rents out his AirBnb bedroom. He flies down to San Diego to winter in Baja.

	Pre	Post
Rent	$2500	$600
Car	$1000	$0
Other Expenses	$2500	$1000
Total	$6000	$1600

Popular neighborhoods include Playas de Tijuana, el Cacho, Hippo-dromo, Zona Rio, and Downtown. Tourist areas with the exception of Zona Rosa are regularly patrolled by police. Petty crime and corruption is pretty common, but mass shootings outside of cartel activity are non-existent – unlike, you know, north of the border.

South towards Rosarito has better weather since it's far enough from the Tijuana valleys with smog and is much safer and a little cheaper. Rosarito is too far for daily border crossings in my opinion but people do it.

Life Aquatic

As you sit in your stable chair reading this on terra firma, there are tens of thousands of people living on boats and many are doing it quite cheaply, just not in hard to find liveaboard marinas at $1/ft of boat per day. Frozen seas present a bit of a challenge for year round liveaboards and any boat owner so the further south the better.

There are TEN advantages that really stick out about the life aquatic:

1. You're almost always going to hit the main criteria of this book being close to coastal infrastructure even broadband internet when you're out on the water.
2. Special rules exist in most counties to ensure free public access to the high tide line so you can just inflate a kayak and go.
3. "Anchoring out" is rent free everywhere and protected by ancient law that local cities don't really have much say over.
4. There are no housing or zoning codes or requirements outside of a marina so you can live in whatever floats. "Seabums" live in inoperable vessels salvaged after hurricanes which is perfectly legal. Freshwater rules are similar.
5. Boats need maintenance and delivery which you can barter living accommodations for or even "watching" an expensive, sitting asset with very little skilled work involved.
6. People give away boats all the time and they are fungible you can buy and sell quickly. Many folks trash their initial boats and don't bother with maintenance.
7. Boats enforce minimalism, discipline, and resourcefulness which are table stakes for living nicely on $1,000 per month.

8. Although theft on boats does happen, you'd still be safer on a boat then anywhere rent is within range of a $1,000 total monthly budget in the US.
9. Boating is social and boat people help each other out.
10. The wind is free and so are fish, crabs and lobster, and are easy to get with boats.

Living on a boat pairs well with all the above strategies discussed so far, even if it means you're sleeping in a canoe in Boston Harbor like Mike Smith[1].

For example, one can join or form a boat share and at ¼ rights with other partners have nights of accomodation secured as other partners will mostly use the boat during the weekends. It's been a while since we've seen X, but if X does one night of dog sit a week and one night roughing it the boat share solves the problem of the missing nights of accommodation - and the members split the maintenance cost and work. You could even mix strategies, by roughing it in an inflate-able kayak or folding canoe that fits in a gym locker.

If in freshwater, a pontoon boat can easily be converted to a spacious houseboat. In the Sacramento Delta, Western lakes and the South this is very common. I have seen some DIY pontoon boats made from plastic barrels that can float a studio sized dwelling.

Houseboats with 3 bedrooms with a dedicated slip can be purchased for under $30k in the Bay Area in prime locations. While slip fees are as high as $2k/mo, so are the room rents and there can be a good opportunity to share costs.

---

[1] https://www.cbsnews.com/news/mariner-makes-waves-living-in-boston-harbor-on-canoe/

Photo credit triumphboats.com

One could also just rent or offer to "watch" a small sailboat such as a pocket cruiser at a mooring field or anchored out. A mooring field is a collection of buoys anchored to the sea floor that boats hook on to so that they don't drift away at night. It's like a parking lot for boats and there's generally a fee to use a mooring buoy. The fee includes secure space at a dock you can use to store your kayak or small boat used to get to land. 'Anchoring out' means you're using your own anchor to keep yourself from drifting away, and is totally free. Anchoring out does not mean you're far from land. In Miami Beach, in many other locations on the intercoastal waterway, you can anchor close enough to land that it's a 5 minute trip. In some cases the water is so shallow, you can just wade through the water to a ladder on a dock.

A photo of the Haulover inlet sandbar in North Miami Beach

A pocket cruiser is a sailboat that can be sailed solo by one person, is generally under 20 ft and can be had for less than $5k. Several popular boats like the Catalina 22, Marshall 16, Com-Pac 16 can be found in most parts of the country - even inland. Of these three, the Catalina 22 is by far the most commonly found used. The type of sailboat you want really depends on your seafaring intent - I assume none because it does take skill just to safely get off the dock. Essentially, you're not sailing in the open ocean here just protected waters like lakes, rivers, and bays or not at all. Basic keelboat certification would be a good investment here.

View of the Catalina 22's inside cabin

If in a warmer climate, like any of the Gulf states or Southern California, you could pitch a tent on top of an 18 ft Hobie Cat . Used Hobie cats range from free to $3k and have 50 sq ft of square use-able space and storage, making these sailboats a great option for Roughing it.

 The key to the Life Aquatic, or really any boating, is to have the smallest boat possible that fits your needs and avoid engines at all costs.

An inflatable kayak fits in a large gym locker and sleeps just like an air mattress but with better privacy.

The Not Stinky Truth

Boats under 25 ft generally won't have a full bathroom - so you'll have to use a port a potty and double bag your excrement out. There is no stink with a composting potty that's sealed. It's illegal to dump your sewage in the water at a marina or within a few miles of the coast. If you have a toilet on board, marinas have pump out stations to handle sewage that is stored in a boat's toilet system.

Water, Electric and Amenities

Most marinas allow day use of their facilities for non-members for a docking fee that might range from $10 to $50 per day. You can dock the boat once per week to re-charge, re-fill, do laundry, etc. You can also join a volunteer-run yacht club for less than $2k per year and use their facilities whenever you want - and possibly barter more accommodation in exchange for being a great volunteer. Joining a yacht club gives you docking privileges at reciprocating yacht clubs in their network.

Small DC powered refrigerators and gas powered stoves are in most boat kitchens. On a smaller boat i.e. less than 25 ft long, you're looking at camping gear essentially for kitchen and bath tasks. So you're stove for example, might be a Coleman double burner you use for camping. Your shower is probably a bucket and hand pump shower wand. Again, less is more here and if the boat is used *just* as a floating bed with minimal sailing the better.

Maintenance

A cheap sailboat (under $5k) will require 100% of its value, and probably more, every year in maintenance and that assumes you do all you can yourself. Small boats are easy to trailer (even dragged with a beach dolly by hand) and can be stored in any backyard or even on public streets for free with valid registration for limited time which greatly reduces storage and maintenance costs when you're mixing strategies. You generally don't need a big truck or SUV to trailer a boat under 20 ft.

Boatyards that charge storage fees tend to be in more isolated places, and people work on them at all hours of the day, so no one is going to bat an eye if you sleep on it occasionally while your boat is 'on the hard.'

Getting Places

Airfare

There are ways to accumulate points, watch fares automatically, and travel at very low prices via air. One strategy that consistently works to make your next flight free is to game the voucher system. Airlines will give you travel credits, hotel stays and free flights if you volunteer to be bumped - but you have to travel during busy times to busy places. You also have to plan your travel around small delays, so that you can act on the voucher. By doing a pay one get one free approach you're essentially receiving 50% off all your travel.

You can also try "skiplagging". This is where you book a multi leg trip where your destination is actually the first connecting city. You bring carry on luggage only and don't complete the other legs of the trip. A direct flight costs more than skiplagging, even though you're essentially getting a direct flight to your intended destination by skiplagging.

Vanpool, car pool

If you've spent years as a drone commuter like me you have probably ignored the car pool signs on the highway. Yet a carpool option can completely remove the need for a car in many cases. In Oakland, folks line up at train stations to get free rides from commuters looking to use the faster HOV lanes over the Bay Bridge going in to San Francisco. Car pool and van pool networks exist in many major cities.

Pre-pandemic, there was a company called Chariot in San Francisco that took folks around in vans, which was a quicker option than a bus but more economical than an Uber. Ultimately, however, even venture capitalists with endless amounts of "air-money" couldn't keep the company afloat as it was such a good deal for their customers.

Bicycle

Photo courtesy of Patrick Hendry, Unsplash

Some folks pay thousands of dollars per week on exclusive bike vacations where they check in to hotels or camp on long distance rides. Why not mix in a week of bike touring every month? A bike can carry a lot of gear and bikes can easily be stashed in bike lockers near public transport where bike lockers exist. Some bike lockers can also function as a small, perfectly located self storage locker. Foldable bikes can be brought on to boats. Bikes can be stashed in the woods with reflectors removed.

Bike routes are very specific though - hills, tunnels and traffic should be avoided and bikeways are more prevalent in some parts of the country. It can be very challenging to plan around water in the West and there is a basic level of investment needed to do bike touring comfortably. However, the investment is far less than vanlife. It's also easier to park a bike than it is a van for several weeks when you're mixing strategies.

The best touring bikes have specific geometry (the angles of the head, top tube, etc...) that make riding long distances comfortable. They also have 'braze ons' or attachment points for racks and tend to have beefier tires than road bikes, yet lighter than mountain bikes. Several bike stores offer free clinics on basic bike maintenance tasks and you'd be wise to skill up on bike maintenance before doing any serious riding.

Depending on the terrain it might make sense to convert a bike to electric via a mid drive conversion kit. The price of e-bikes is falling, but I still see $500 convert kits on a good hybrid as an option. The motor in a mid drive system is near the crank pedal and assists on uphills - mid drive is considered the most efficient and least obtrusive. The extra battery weight could be worth it if recharge stations are available every 50 miles or so.

Boat Delivery

Photo courtesy of Hassan Nizan / Unsplash

Another way to get places for free is to deliver boats from one port to another or to acquire basic seafaring skills and then act as a deckhand or skipper on a yacht. In Fort Lauderdale, Florida, and in most larger ports with a vacation scene (Port Washington, NY etc...), you'll find lots of single men and women or even couples who sail around the world this way, disembarking at European ports to work for a season as guides for sea kayaking tours, snorkeling tours, or parasailing trips. On larger power yachts, the boats are basically run by crew with the owners absent 90% of the time. If you're a dive master, or have other vacation-y skills like photography / water sports enthusiast, or coast guard certifications, you're in high demand. This is a fantastic way to get hours needed for a captain's license. Return fares are frequently offered. Couples welcome!

New York to Florida is a very common boat delivery route in winter (boats have to be removed from the ocean during freezes) and boat deliveries to the Mediterranean are also popular. The skill level is very subjective and you'll find being able to cook and do basic maintenance are about all that's needed.

Other Delivery

There are also websites to help match you to folks who need a car or pet driven across country. For pets, there may be special licensing and you'd need your own vehicle - but pet fare is a great way to subsidize your travel.

Free Money

Freeganism

There's a movement out there of folks who neither accept nor give paper money. It's called freeganism and while some of their practices are a bit fringe or dare I say *cringe* (dumpster diving for food), it's an interesting philosophy built on freeriding the main cash economy. Do you really need to use money to get what you want? If you've only got $1,000 a month, it's a valid question to ask. There's a host of resources and techniques that are discussed on freegan forums, Facebook Groups and freegan living sites on the Internet. One guy, Daniel Suelo, has been doing it for years and wrote a book on his approach to living without money.

Public Benefit Programs

If you've saved enough to generate $1,000 per month in income for life before you're 40, you can check any ethical considerations of using public programs at the door. You're just getting your money back. Even if you weren't fortunate enough to cough up 20%+ of your income to Uncle Sam, your decades of consumption has likely filled the coffers of various government agencies along the way as money multiplies throughout the economy.

At $1,000 per month income you may qualify for a lot of state, Federal, county and city level programs in the US even if you're *not* a US citizen. The key is understanding what is counted in personal assets, if assets are considered at all.

Here's a rundown of what's available as of July 2022 from the

Federal government. I am not a public benefits expert at all so you should consult a social worker to help you navigate the maze of money the government will throw at you. This is very much a summary of what the program is and eligibility.

1. Medicaid. Healthcare including emergency, preventive and reproductive. For lawfully present immigrants and citizens, pregnant women, seniors, parents, SSI recipients, adults under 65 not living in certain states. There are asset and income ceilings. The lowest ceiling is $841/mo for Singles in some states. In California there is no asset test. In New York one can have up to $17k liquid assets. What's countable as an asset varies.
2. SSI. $500/mo+ for citizens who don't work and certain non-citizens. Max $2,000 in personal assets allowed. Food stamps not included in assets. The basic requirement is age over 65 or disabled. SSI does not require physical disability. You have to have limited income or resources to apply and can't reside outside the 50 states for more than 30 days.
3. Earned Income Tax Credit. Starts at $1500+ /year for citizens and certain non citizens with earned income. Earned income must be under $21k for singles with no kids.
4. WIC. Benefits for Pregnant women, infants and children
5. SNAP. Food stamps delivered on a debit card. Can easily accumulate to thousands of dollars worth. Certain items, like beer and hot food, are not eligible. Accepted at farmer's markets.
6. Cellphones[1]. If you're eligible for any of the programs above. There are additional programs not listed above, such as tribal related programs, that can also qualify you. The offers vary by state, but in the Bay Area a household of 2 qualifies at $32,500.

---

[1] https://www.freegovernmentcellphones.net/states/florida-government-cell-phone-providers

7. Section 8 - Any type of housing is eligible - duplexes, apartments, etc...as long as it passes an inspection. The program is administered by local housing authorities at the county level. Typically you have to make less than 50% of the median income in the county to qualify, with most funds going to those under 30%, and there are waitlists (which periodically open and close) with local preferences. For example, people fleeing domestic violence or displaced by natural disasters may be prioritized. The program delivers coupons to provide to a landlord where the government pays the landlord directly about 70% of the rent and utilities. Again, eligibility varies by income level and household size and every county's application process and preferences is different. Also, there are affordable housing options without any government programs available throughout the country. Waitlists and income restrictions apply.

X has been renting out his 3rd room and now only earns a few thousand a year and qualifies for the EITC, a free cellphone, and utilities. His other expenses drop to $500.

	Pre	Post
Rent	$2500	$-500
Car	$1000	$0
Other Expenses	$2500	$500
Total	$6000	$0

The value of food, health insurance, internet and the EITC alone are over $1,000/mo for Singles. Add in Section 8 in a high cost of living area and the value grows to past $3,000 a month. Most benefits in this list are intertwined with state level programs, which offer more.

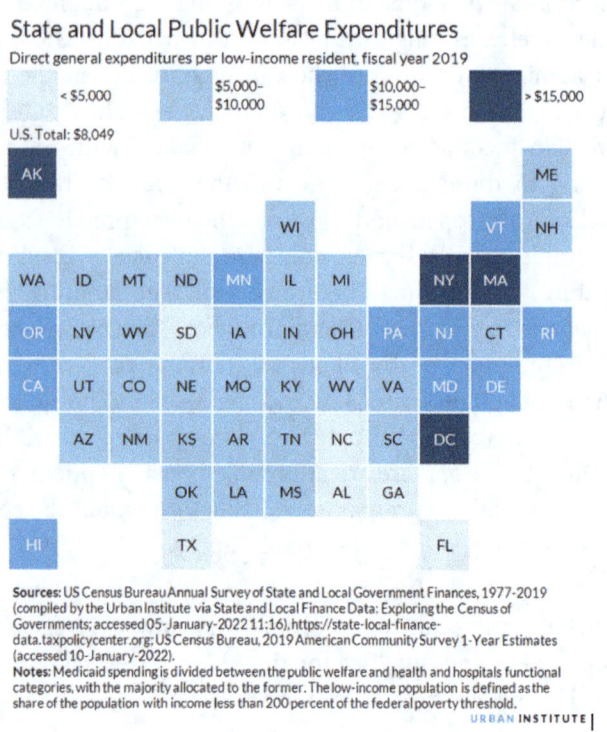

State and Local Public Welfare Expenditures

Direct general expenditures per low-income resident, fiscal year 2019

| | < $5,000 | | $5,000–$10,000 | | $10,000–$15,000 | | > $15,000 |

U.S. Total: $8,049

Sources: US Census Bureau Annual Survey of State and Local Government Finances, 1977-2019 (compiled by the Urban Institute via State and Local Finance Data: Exploring the Census of Governments; accessed 05-January-2022 11:16), https://state-local-finance-data.taxpolicycenter.org; US Census Bureau, 2019 American Community Survey 1-Year Estimates (accessed 10-January-2022).

Notes: Medicaid spending is divided between the public welfare and health and hospitals functional categories, with the majority allocated to the former. The low-income population is defined as the share of the population with income less than 200 percent of the federal poverty threshold.

URBAN **INSTITUTE** |

Figure 2. Free money per state

Even Southern states[2] are kicking in $400/mo per low income resident. If we take Miami Dade County, $40 million has been earmarked for about 4,000 homeless people in the Homeless Trust, roughly $10,000 per person per year. While most of the resources are centered around sheltering, there are over 100 services[3] funded by the trust. The city of South Miami at one point provided the equivalent of free ride sharing with its on demand shuttle service[4].

---

[2]https://www.urban.org/policy-centers/cross-center-initiatives/state-and-local-finance-initiative/state-and-local-backgrounders/public-welfare-expenditures

[3]https://www.homelesstrust.org/homeless-trust/about-us/home.page

[4]https://www.southmiamifl.gov/DocumentCenter/View/4697/South-Miami-South-Miami-Pamphlet---November-2020

At the city level, San Francisco is probably the most generous. At a whopping $60,000 of expenditures per homeless person, San Francisco - a city that is only 7 miles wide - is doling out the equivalent of what a fully employed middle class person with a college degree in Sparks, Nevada makes. Sparks is a bedroom community in Reno. Note, San Francisco's city budget does not include the *additional* $1 billion that is funneled to homeless people through not for profits every year in San Francisco. While this money is not cash received by homeless people (a lot of it goes to salaries to keep the hearts bleeding) it shows you that per low income resident there's money on the table for *you*.

For example, Dog care[5] , legal services[6], and even travel assistance are available.

Free Food and Alcohol

By far the best way to get free food is the SNAP program if you qualify, but there are restrictions on what you can buy. Food that are hot at point of sale, vitamins, any vice purchases (beer, cigarettes), and pet foods are not eligible.

Meetup.com is a great website for community building. In large cities, it is common for companies to recruit talent and support the mostly tech community through meetups where beer and pizza are provided. In college, I would occasionally entertain some religious zealot intent on converting me for the free food.

What should you spend on food? According to the graph below, about $100 a week.

---

[5]https://www.petsofthehomeless.org/get-help/find-locations/paws-san-francisco/
[6]https://sfserviceguide.org/

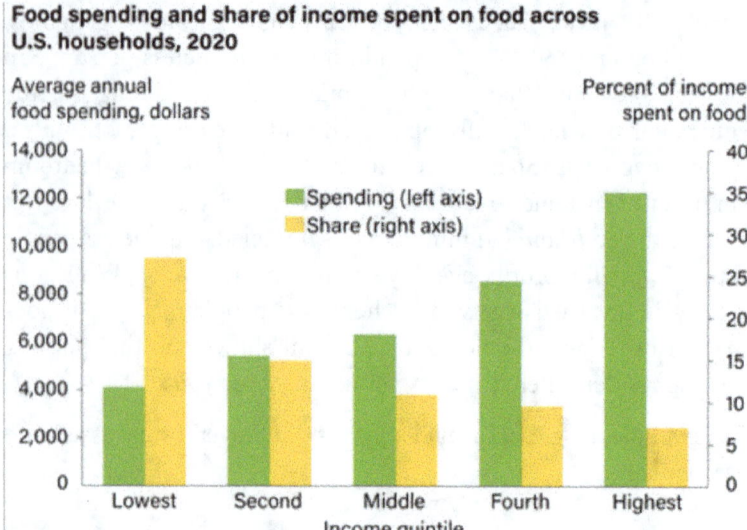

Food spending and share of income spent on food across U.S. households, 2020

Figure 3. Food Budget

But with food banks in every city, food stamps from SNAP and not for profits doling out food, your individual food budget should be *zero*. To put things into perspective, Marin County in California is one of the top ten wealthiest counties in the country and 1% of the population get meals delivered free from the SF-Marin Foodbank program.

There is no shortage of warm food in the US.

Free & Deeply Discounted Hotel Stays

It's quite possible you could find 4 nights of accommodation somewhere cheap. Major chains typically offer the 5th night free somewhere else. If you use a hotel credit card, you might have free breakfast through lounge benefits. You can also buy gift cards through hotels.com or marketplaces like giftcardwiki.com to stack discounts. Overall, it takes research and planning to take advantage of these offers but the savings can be compelling over the long run. If you run a travel blog with a social media presence, you could also trade nights for reviews aka the influencer model.

Conclusion

My goal with this book was to illustrate how its possible to live on $1,000 per month in the United States if you just rethink a few basic things, like how long you stay in one place or if you stop working and spend more time outside. Every day, millions of Americans live on $1,000 month budget and they're not doing anything fun - its hard, because they're trying to live a life that is increasingly harder to do as a solo unit. They are often successful through deep family connections and community ties.

Community ties cannot be understated. While nomadism and adventurous self reliance are themes in this book that is only my bias in achieving a $1,000/mo goal. Certainly staying in place and building community ties is very doable with these strategies in any major metropolitan area.

www.ingramcontent.com/pod-product-compliance
Lightning Source LLC
Chambersburg PA
CBHW062246290526
45794CB00006B/2428